Across Golden Hills

Meditations on California Oaks

Contact: www.williamguion.com • bill@williamguion.com

Design direction by Linda Herman and Glyph Publishing Arts
1st printing 2013 by Taylor Specialty Books, Dallas, Texas
Type: Pastonchi MT Standard and Titling

ISBN-13: 978-0-615-29952-5

CONSERVING CALIFORNIA'S OAKS

The oak became America's official favorite tree in December 2004 by Congressional Act. This occurred after millions of people from all walks of life cast their votes in a National Arbor Day Foundation contest to discover America's most beloved tree.

California's oak trees are a familiar sight across the state, valued and cherished by many. Oak woodlands and oak-dotted savannahs are among the most beloved views of the state's varied landscapes.

The most common and widespread species are the coast live oak (Quercus agrifolia), the blue oak (Q. douglasii), and the valley oak (Q. lobata), followed by the canyon live oak (Q. chrysolepis), California black oak (Q. kelloggii), interior live oak (Quercus wislizenii), the Engelmann oak (Q. engelmannii) and the Oregon white oak (Q. garryana).

Throughout California's history, people have lived among the oaks, raised families in homes shaded by oaks, worked and played around these generous natural and cultural icons. Oaks have played a crucial role in supporting the health and well being of people, plants, and animals across the state for decades. California's critical watersheds count on oaks to hold soil and filter the water supply needed for a growing population. Oak woodlands – those densely wooded areas where the dominant trees are oaks – support a surprising variety of wildlife.

In the Central Coast range, as many as 2000 species of animals and plants living in and around oaks are dependant on the delicate ecological mosaic created by their presence. These numbers include more than 50 species of mammals, 200 species of birds, 29 species of reptiles and amphibians, 260 species of bees and butterflies and 600 species of vascular plants.[1]

Although California is blessed with more varieties of oak species than anywhere else in the United States, conservation of oaks has never been more important. As oaks have been cleared for agricultural expansion and land-gobbling development, the state now leads the nation with more species protected under the Federal Endangered Species Act (ESA) than any other state.[2] Altering the natural balance of nature and oak ecological systems has a dramatic impact on the ability of the land to support life on many levels.

Like ripples in a pond, the changes in oak habitat have

far-reaching effects on surrounding life.

Over many years, responsible Californians have consistently stepped up to ensure a state of beauty and biodiversity. According to the California Protected Areas Database (CPAD), the total area of protected wilderness lands is approximately 49 million acres, or 46.7% of the state. This includes national and state parks, monuments, preserves and wildlife refuges, conservation easements protecting private lands and other protected areas.

Many partnerships between state and federal government agencies, non-profit conservation organizations, and community and business groups invest their expertise, time, and funding to ensure that future generations will inherit the rich diversity that marks the state. Citizens have consistently voted to support this important work by approving funds to protect the state's natural capital. We must keep in mind, however, that thousands of acres of critical oak habitat are privately owned and currently lack protection. There is still a great deal of work to be done on behalf of conserving the oak ecosystem.

More and more people are spending time on trails, in parks and special places. Their health and well being benefit from the transformative power and peace that is gained from personally experiencing California's green infrastructure.

Protecting these resources is a wise investment that will pay big dividends for many years to come.

Janet Cobb
Executive Officer
California Oaks & California Wildlife Foundation
www.californiawildlifefoundation.org, www.californiaoaks.org

NOTES

[1] www.bigsurlandtrust.org
[2] *Conservation of Oak Woodlands – Recognizing the Values;* by Gregory A. Giusti

For more information on California oaks:
• California Oaks – www.californiaoaks.org
• California Oak Woodlands Conservation Program – www.wcb.ca.gov/oaks

For landowners who want to know what they can do to conserve their oaks, read *Living Among the Oaks. A Management Guide for Landowners.* Copies may be obtained from the University of California Cooperative Extension, Natural Resources Program, 163 Mulford Hall, Berkeley, CA 94720, or call (510) 643-5428.

3

Santa Lucia ridges with oaks and chaparral, late afternoon light

A VIEW ACROSS GOLDEN HILLS

My earliest memories of California are of the rolling golden hills of the Santa Lucia Range of Central California. I was on the last leg of a flight to Monterey where I was enrolled in a photography workshop hosted by the Friends of Photography in Carmel.

Through my airplane window, I watched mile after mile of gold and ochre ridges drifting slowly by, thousands of feet below. Rounded knolls, savannahs and canyons — all dotted with oak trees and washed in honey-colored afternoon light.

Fifteen years later I returned to work and live in Monterey after as many years photographing the live oaks and landscapes of my home state of Louisiana. The challenge for me, in an area that had been photographed so frequently and so well by others, was to find a way to say something new, something that reflected my personal experience of this place. And to express that in a way that was not just a facsimile of what others had already done.

Though the topography was unfamiliar, the oaks were old friends. So that's where I began.

I took to the rolling hills of the nearby Santa Lucia and Diablo Ranges and followed the animal paths and hiking trails. I wandered among the oaks, sat on their roots, and observed their changing moods in different light and different seasons. Slowly, I began to hear their whispers. And I let them guide me in finding a way to see and photograph them.

My time spent with the oaks has had unexpected effects. It's as though something of the character of the trees rubs off on one who seeks their company. For me, the oaks have broadened my perspective on life and my place within the complex fabric of the ecosystems I inhabit and participate in.

With each new contact with the natural world, I gain a deep and renewed feeling of peace, humility and wonder. Over time, I've even come to understand more clearly my purpose in this life and my fascination with the oaks.

But see for yourself. Spend an hour or a day in nature. Put yourself under the inflence of earth, trees and sky. Soak it all in and let it work its magic.

— *William Guion*

4

WE NEED WILD COUNTRY

Something will have gone out of us as a people
if we ever let the remaining wilderness
be destroyed...

We simply need that wild country
available to us,
even if we never do more
than drive to its edge and look in.

— Wallace Stegner
author & environmentalist

Blue oak in fog, study 23, Santa Lucia Range, Carmel Valley

Valley oak on ridge, morning light, Santa Lucia Range

ONLY A GREEN THING

The tree which moves some to tears of joy
is in the eyes of others
only a green thing that stands in the way.

Some see nature all ridicule and deformity...
and some scarce see nature at all.

But to the eyes of the man of imagination,
nature is imagination itself.

— William Blake
English poet

STILL BEAUTIFUL

In nature, nothing is perfect
and everything is perfect.

Trees can be contorted,
bent in weird ways,
and they're still beautiful.

— Alice Walker
American author & poet

Coast live oak silhouette, Santa Lucia Range

11

Valley oak savannah, afternoon light, Santa Lucia Range

THE LAST MILE

All endeavor calls for the ability
to tramp the last mile,
shape the last plan,
endure the last hour's toil.

The fight to the finish spirit
is the one characteristic we must possess
if we are to face the future as finishers.

— Henry David Thoreau
writer & naturalist

PERSPECTIVE

Climb up on some hill at sunrise.
Everybody needs perspective
once in a while —
you'll find it there.

— Robb Sagendorph
Former editor, Yankee Magazine

Coast live oak silhouette, twilight, Santa Lucia Range

15

Oak and river rocks, Big Sur

SERMONS IN STONES

And this, our life,
exempt from public haunt,
finds tongues in trees,
books in the running brooks,
sermons in stones,
and good in everything.
I would not change it.

—William Shakespeare
from "As You Like It."

TELL THE WORLD

We must get beyond textbooks,
go out into the bypaths...
and tell the world
the glories of our journey.

— John Hope Franklin
American historian

Oak snag and summer grasses, Santa Lucia Range

19

Deer trail through oak woodlands, afternoon, Santa Lucia Range

MORE THAN WHAT IS IN BOOKS

Reading about nature is fine,
but if a person walks in the woods
and listens carefully,
he can learn more than what is in books,
for they speak with the voice of God.

— *George Washington Carver*
scientist & educator

21 A SINGLE TREE

How beautiful, when a whole tree is like one great scarlet fruit
full of ripe juices, every leaf from lowest limb to topmost spire,
all aglow, especially if you look toward the sun!

What more remarkable object can there be in the landscape?
A single tree becomes thus the crowning beauty
of some meadowy vale,
and the expression of the whole surrounding forest
is at once more spirited for it.

— John Muir
naturalist & author

Valley oak, summer afternoon, Santa Lucia Range

23

Ranch road and oak savannah, Santa Lucia Range

THE ROAD'S BEGINNING

He who chooses the beginning of a road
chooses the place it leads to.
It is the means that determine the end.

— Harry Emerson Fosdick
American pastor

IN SOME MYSTERIOUS WAY

In some mysterious way
woods have never seemed to me
to be static things.

In physical terms,
I move through them;
yet in metaphysical ones,
they seem to move through me.

— John Fowles
English novelist

Blue oak in fog, study 1, Santa Lucia Range

Oaks and fence with distant hills, afternoon light, Santa Lucia Range

THE BLUE DREAM OF SKY

I thank you God
for this most amazing day,
for the leaping greenly spirits of trees,
and for the blue dream of sky,
and for everything which is natural,
which is infinite,
which is yes.

— e.e. cummings
poet

ALONE WITH THE HEAVENS

The best remedy for those who are afraid,
lonely or unhappy is to go outside,
somewhere where they can be quiet,
alone with the heavens, nature and God.

Because only then does one feel
that all is as it should be.

— Anne Frank
Jewish holocaust survivor

Oak savannah, afternoon haze, Santa Lucia Range

Valley oak silhouette, twilight, Santa Lucia Range

STAND IN THE OPEN

The strongest oak of the forest
is not the one
that is protected from the storm
and hidden from the sun.

It's the one that stands in the open
where it is compelled to struggle
for its existence
against the wind
and rains
and scorching sun.

— *Napoleon Hill*
American author

THE CHALLENGE

We need wilderness preserved —
as much of it as is still left,
and as many kinds —
because it was the challenge
against which our character as a people was formed.

The reminder and reassurance that it is still there
is good for our spiritual health
even if we never once in ten years set foot in it.

— Wallace Stegner
author & environmentalist

Valley and blue oak savannah, afternoon, Santa Lucia Range

Blue oak study, summer light, Santa Lucia Range

THE LISTENING HEAVEN

Trees are the Earth's endless effort
to speak to the listening heaven.

— Rabindranath Tagore
writer, poet

UNDERSTANDING

Look deep into nature,
and then you will understand
everything better.

— *Albert Einstein*
physicist

Trail through blue oak woodland, summer, Diablo Range

39

Oak grove in fog, study 24, Santa Lucia Range

THE AIR SHARES ITS SPIRIT

All things share the same breath —
the beast, the tree, the man.

The air shares its spirit
with all the life it supports.

— Chief Seattle
Chief of Suquamish tribe

ANY ROAD

If you do not know where you are going,
any road will take you there.

— Sterling Holloway
American actor

Ranch road through oak savannah, Santa Lucia Range

43

Weathered ranch fence and oak savannah, afternoon, Santa Lucia Range

NOT A LOVER OF LAWNS

I am not a lover of lawns.
Rather would I see daisies
in their thousands,
ground ivy, hawkweed,
and even the hated plantain
with tall stems,
and dandelions with splendid flowers
and fairy down,
than the too-well-tended lawn.

— *William H. Hudson*
author and naturalist

COLORS

Nature always wears
the colors of the spirit.

— Ralph Waldo Emerson
American essayist

Blue oak hilltop, summer afternoon, Santa Lucia Range

Interior live oak, Santa Lucia Range

THE NATURE OF THINGS

For in the true nature of things,
if we rightly consider,
every green tree is far more glorious
than if it were made of gold and silver.

— Martin Luther
Professor of theology

A COMMON LANGUAGE

Like music and art,
love of nature is a common language
that can transcend political
or social boundaries.

— Jimmy Carter
39th U.S. President

Oak limbs and grazing deer, twilight, Santa Lucia Range

51

Oak savannah study 7, Santa Lucia Range

THE CHEERING LIGHT

The mind,
in proportion as it is cut off
from free communication with nature,
with revelation, with God, with itself,
loses its life,
just as the body droops
when debarred from the air
and the cheering light from heaven.

— William Ellery Channing
American Unitarian preacher

A FOCUSING LENS

The environment is where we all meet;
where all have a mutual interest;
it is the one thing all of us share.

It is not only a mirror of ourselves,
but a focusing lens on what we can become.

— Lady Bird Johnson
conservationist

Blue oak study 15, Santa Lucia Range

Oak savannah study 5, Santa Lucia Range

YOUR NATURE

The goal of life
is to make your heartbeat
match the beat of the universe,
to match your nature with Nature.

— Joseph Campbell
American mythologist

UNHURRIED

Nature does not hurry,
yet everything is accomplished.

— Lao Tzu
Chinese philosopher

Golden hills with oaks and chaparral, afternoon, Santa Lucia Range

Coast live oak, ridgetop, Carmel Valley

WHAT WE KNOW

Miracles are not contrary to nature,
but only contrary
to what we know about nature.

— Saint Augustine of Hippo
Catholic bishop in Africa

NOTHING IS LACKING

Human subtlety will never devise
an invention more beautiful,
more simple or more direct
than does nature,
because in her inventions
nothing is lacking,
and nothing is superfluous.

– Leonardo da Vinci
artist & inventor

Three coast live oaks in grove, backlit, Santa Lucia Range

Oak woodland study, afternoon light, Diablo Range

UNDER THE INFLUENCE

The lasting pleasures of contact
with the natural world
are not reserved for scientists
but are available to anyone
who will place himself
under the influence of earth,
sea and sky and their amazing life.

– Rachel Carson
conservationist & author

EVERY HOUR

I love to think of nature
as an unlimited broadcasting station,
through which God speaks to us every hour,
if we will only tune in.

— *George Washington Carver*
scientist and educator

Blue oak hilltop, summer light, Santa Lucia Range

Blue oak study 3, Diablo Range

ON LOAN

The earth, the air, the land and the water
are not an inheritance from our forefathers
but on loan from our children.

So we have to hand it over to them
at least as it was handed over to us.

— Mohandas K. Ghandi
Indian nationalist

THE REAL MAGICIAN

I knew, of course,
that trees and plants had roots,
stems, bark, branches and foliage
that reached up toward the light.

But I was coming to realize
that the real magician was light itself.

— Edward Steichen
photographer

Valley oak hillside, summer light, Santa Lucia foolthills

Oaks along deer trail, Diablo Range

SEEK RELIEF IN THE TRAIL

Whenever the pressure
of our complex city life thins my blood
and numbs my brain,
I seek relief in the trail;
and when I hear the coyote wailing
to the yellow dawn,
my cares fall from me —
I am happy.

— Hamlin Garland
American novelist

EACH GIFT OF NATURE

The ground we walk on,
the plants and creatures,
the clouds above
constantly dissolving into new formations —
each gift of nature possesses its own radiant energy,
bound together by cosmic harmony.

— Ruth Bernhard
photographer

Leaning blue oak, Santa Lucia Range

Valley oak on ridge, late light, Santa Lucia Range

WE RECEIVE STRENGTH

Every living person and thing
responds to beauty.
We all thirst for it.
We receive strength and renewal
by seeing stirring and satisfying sites.

— Rachael Carson
conservationist & author

A MIRROR

Nature holds up a mirror
so we can see more clearly
the ongoing processes of growth,
renewal and transformation
in our lives.

— Mary Ann Brussat
Spirituality & Practice

Oak and distant hills, near Atascadero

ACKNOWLEDGEMENTS

Merci beaucoups to the many people who helped bring this book into form. First and foremost, thanks to the partners of Blue Oak Capital, LLC of Palo Alto, for their continued patronage and support. Thanks to Janet Cobb and the staff of the California Wildlife Foundation for their dedication to protecting and preserving California's wilderness areas and the plants and animals that rely on those wild spaces to live. They are true caretakers of the land and deserve our full support. And warm thanks to Linda Herman of Glyph Publishing Arts for her design direction for *Across Golden Hills*.

Thanks to the staff of the Santa Lucia Conservancy and the Santa Lucia Preserve for their openness in sharing the rolling golden hills and oaks under their stewardship in Carmel Valley where several of these images were made. And great praise and appreciation to the national, state, and regional parks, park rangers and volunteer staff from across California's Central Coast and the entire state for their tireless work to preserve the wilderness lands under their protection — many, *many* thanks.

To the many authors, conservationists, scientists, educators and outspoken individuals who see and appreciate the value of wilderness and whose writings I've quoted to accompany the images in this book, I offer my gratitude and appreciation.

Special thanks to: Alice Walker for permission to use her quote; to the family of Robb Sagendorph, former editor of *Yankee Magazine* and the *Old Farmer's Almanac*; to Random House for the use of Wallace Stegner's quotes; to Mary Ann Brussat of Spirituality & Practice; to Harper Collins for the use of Harry Fosdick's quote; to the Sierra Club for the use of John Muir quotes; and the John Hope Franklin Center for the use of his quote.